Watershed

About the book

Watershed collects three albums of lyrics about whatever happened before and after passing from one hell to another, about how to survive death and about how to move on after death – written in English by j. t. baka in the years of 2018 and 2019.

About the author

j. t. baka published previously a couple of books in German under the pen names of Otaru Tomis and David Jordan. *Watershed. Another Three Albums of English Lyrics* is his second publication in English only after *She Was. Three Albums of English Lyrics* in 2017. Check out his website for more details about him and his books: https://otaru-tomis.jimdo.com.

j. t. baka

Watershed

Another

Three Albums of English Lyrics

Impressum

Redaktionsschluss: 01.02.2019.

Fotos : Simon Wagenschütz.

©2019
Herstellung und Verlag: BoD - Books on Demand, Norderstedt.

ISBN-13: 9783748126003.

Contents

Album

비

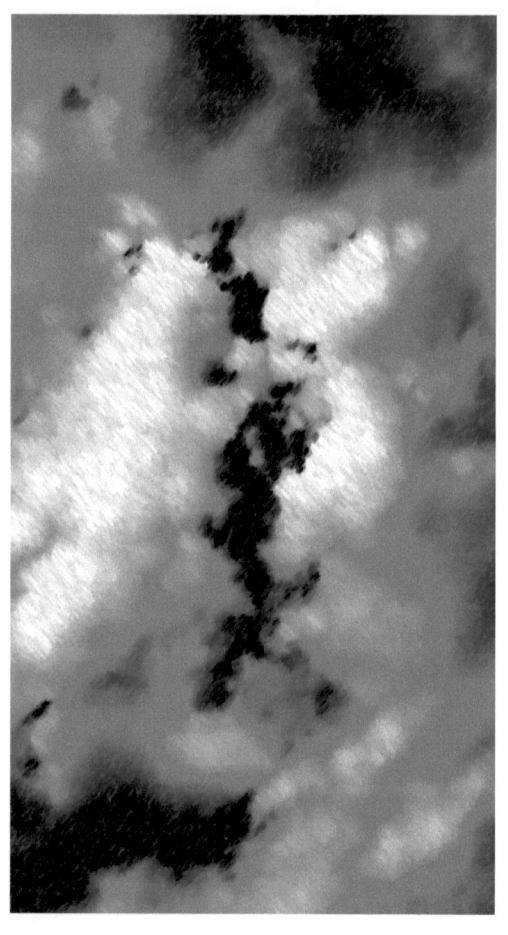

[lost]

I am

still here

I am

still there

I am still

gone   雨

it was

the spring

without the cherry blossoms'

little helpers

their friends and admirers

the cherry blossoms were

showing off their beauty

all in vain

they withered away

leaving nothing behind

numb and barren

but wait

it wasn't

that spring

that spring came

later

remember

the spring after

I've lost

both of you

it was

that spring

the spring

of no cherry blossoms   雨

Meta-Ebene 51

pardon

my german

I wanted to write about

you

but then I realized

that

when I did it once

before

back then

it cost me

cost

me

a lot

and for what

I am not even able

to make money off my pain

so what's the use

what's the excuse

to get

over it

how so

if I'm crashed

by it

buried deep down

at the bottom

of the sea

listening to the deep sea diver sounds

sticky with rejection

sticky

with me   雨

sound fishing

the shadow

escaped through a black hole

into the mirror

still staring at me

he laughed without a sound

until I

shot him

in the dark

turning into flames

he laughed even harder

until his laughter

turned

and burst free

shattering the mirror

shattering me   雨

racing

along the edge of a scream

howling

a wedge in your dream

until

you SCREAM

of pain

for my gain

'til there is

no restrain

in my pain   雨

a child is crying

embraced by madness

encased in sadness

stricken by terror

tears and horror

full of sorrow

pumped up by death

without recess

hollowed and then

swallowed by

numbness

silenced

no child is crying   雨

interior shots

a child is crying

acting

on instincts

alone

until dissolving into a siren's

howl

encased in reinforced

concrete

no child is crying   雨

sticky with me

a child is crying

no wonder

then

that it never worked

with those

I

really loved

with all of my heart

with all of my being

no child is crying   雨

exterior shots

standing on the cliff of sounds

staring at the fog of white noise

beneath my feet

wondering

who was calling the shots

I hear

zeroing in on me

until I am

falling

losing myself

in the mist

spilling deaf dreams

running wild

all around

the sound

of heaven

until I

hit

rock bottom   雨

safe space

dancing

on the top of a pen

sharper than the sharpest knife

slicing

open the space around your heart

cutting

off your heart's connections

retrieving

your pulsating heart

cleansing

the wound

with the acid of unwritten confessions

sterilizing

the chasm

with the poison of unsaid vows

filling

the hole

with the remains of hope's rotten corpse

closing

the void

with a love aborted

and then

feasting on my still screaming heart

burning it

turning it   雨

ghosts of the past

aghast

vast is the ether

but that doesn't mean

we were together

oh heather

jamming along

and singing to my song

without knowing

you were dead wrong

mr wong

why not lying

before dying

it's better than crying

mee-ling

my darling

off we go

to the show

of no tomorrow

so without sorrow

we're done

mr fang

honk honk

that's no way

to end a song

so long

sunny

you were not funny   雨

because

I wanted

to write about

something

I wanted

to write about

us

but

I couldn't come up

with something

anything

clever

雨

dharma for two

you didn't know

what happened

you didn't know

me

you just

didn't

and I didn't know

what happened either

as I didn't know

you either

dancing for two

I just

didn't

so we didn't know

what happened

we didn't know

each other

we just

didn't   雨

Album

self-mutilation

bando

if you are

just looking for a fling

all you need is bling-bling

and you will be king

for a night

if that's alright

for you lou

but if you zing

your heart starts to swing

and you might start to sing

as well oh swell

because if you zing

the world starts to sing

as well oh swell

following another tune

than before

until you feel a chill

that might kill

the zing

so that you will never

ever

sing

and your heart stops

to swing

and there will never be

a wedding ring

or any such romantic thing

you poor ol' thing

just death

bad luck

what's

the devil's

most effective weapon of torture

giving

you a choice

and too

much time to decide

but

such is life

dream

cherry blossoms

swaying in the wind

burning

wisdom

don't look

for an answer

if it doesn't change

what is

reality

the cherry tree is swaying

in the light breeze

of spring

it's sending off

its blossoms

the cherry blossoms

traveling on the southern winds

are carried higher and higher

until kissed by the sun

turning up in flames

they spiral

down

burning bright

they dissolve into ashen flakes

of a love

killed

survival

see the day

see the day

as a day

day by day

see the day

as it is

day by day

it is a day

just

one day

a day

like today

or

day after day

a day

like tomorrow

'cause

tomorrow is a day

as well

but it will be

a day

like a day of tomorrow

so

tomorrow

will be

a new day

then

and you

see yourself

as a new man

then

day after day

as the man of tomorrow

day after day

it may

make life easier then

day by day

day after day

you see

surrender

today

was a day of celebration

today

was my big day

today

I turned 40

and

I got me a dog

a cute little puppy

just

for me

for today and tomorrow

and every day

after

tomorrow

to love

condolences

here

we are

and

here

it is

proudly

presented

Death & Destruction

your

CONSOLATION PRICE

a love story [Bonus]

I am looking

around and

see there is

someone

not to be overlooked

while

I am looking you

over

I am checking you

out

while

you are looking me

over

you are checking me

out

while

we are working things

out

while

we are getting

over

some humps

we get to know each other better

and better

until

it's our

big night

I am

coming over to you

where

we are

all over each other

over and over and

over again

time and again

over and over and

over again

until

you

are coming over to me

where

we are

all over each other

over and over and

over again

time and again

over and over and

over again

back and forth

forth and back

over

to you

over

to me

give and

take take

and give

that's how it

works between us

until

it's not working

between us

any longer

until

it's

over

and we are forced

to get

over each other

to get

over us

[over and out]

Album

Snow.Falling

A Sacrifice

인생사진

<u>Table of Contents</u>

stranded

in a wasteland

lost

in a dreamscape

hollowed shadows

a foreigner

to myself

again and again and again

again

reach for the sky

don't let your fate

decide your destiny

don't follow your

fellow man

don't listen to their

screaming

start dreaming

set course

set sail

and follow the light

follow your star

the chase

taking our chances

looking for

what's looking for us

cruising foreign seas

over unknown shallows

taking our chances

looking for

what's looking for us

crossing the abyss

into the unknown

taking our chances

looking for

what's looking for us

sailing along

the coastline of foreign lands

looking for

what's looking for us

taking

our chances

looking

for the next horizon of endless possibilities

looking

for the next change of heart

trapped

suddenly

an ice storm

is closing in

on us

desperate

we are trying

to outrun

its fury

relentless

its chasing us

without mercy

forcing us

into a fjord

and

closing the fjord's entrance

with a solid wall of ice

closing us

in

for the time being

hope

surrounded by a range of mountains

clad in white

the fjord

looks like the end of our journey

the only exit

closed shut

by an unbreachable gate

set there by the ruler of this world

the storm is still raging its war

right above us

high in the sky

the temperature is dropping

by the second

turning the water and our ship

in a motionless sculpture of ice

lost in time

the world around us

drowns in an all-consuming white darkness

but

for one

flickering light

on one of the mountain tops

decision (crossroads)

the temperature

dropping even further

the ice closing

in on us more and more

the man

panicking

running around

searching

for a way out

of this death trap

while I am focusing

on the flickering light

on one of the mountain tops

zeroing in on it

I am trying to force the light

force the light

to shine

to shine steadily

to shine bright

to shine brighter

and brighter and brighter and brighter

I am trying to push the light

push the light

to come close

to come closer

and closer and closer and closer

just a bit closer

just a bit

just

at first

nothing is happening

but then

I see the light

soaring

down the mountain

bright and clear

it's swooping down

on us

bright and steady

it's growing stronger and stronger

growing bright like a star bright

like a face bright

like a face with a smile

shining bright

full of light

a smile

right in front of me

belonging to a woman

a woman

reaching out to me

a touch so gentle

like a kiss full of promise

don't let your fate

decide your destiny

don't follow your

fellow men

she says

exploding

in a kaleidoscope of light

I wake with a start

covered in

a blanket of ice

surrounded by my fellow men

lost to the ice queen's dream

the light on the mountain top

still there

bright and steady

a beacon

in this black ocean of white death

don't let your fate

decide your destiny

she said

follow your dream

she said

follow the light

together

careful

so careful

I make my way off the ship

careful

so very careful

I make my way to the shore

expecting with every step to

break through the ice and drown

carefully

I climb on land

sliding so often back

again and again

until finally

I face nothing

but a huge mountain right in front of me

I take one last look back

to the ship

to see it crashed by the ice

smashed to pieces

careful

so very very careful

I start to climb

following the light

still there

high up in the darkness

but at the same time right in front of me

as well

gritting teeth

go on or go down

I hear myself saying

fighting my way up a mountain

made of ice and wind

singing of death

trying to force my will

on the mountain

the mountain forces its will

on me

making it more and more difficult

with every step and every breath

to keep track

of the light and of me

when a fist of rock and ice hits

all I can do

is to let go

falling

falling

falling

like snow

drifting

without direction

spiraling

down

until

until

I hear

hear

her

her

voice

again

don't let your fate

decide your destiny

she says

don't follow your

fellow men to the other side

into the endless cold of an ice star

she says

follow your dream

she says

I blink my eyes

open

and see

it's still

there

the light

high up in the mountains

and right in front of me

at the same time

I am

I am not

alone

in this

not at all

no

follow me

she said

echoes of vanishing

snow

still falling

still fighting

for my life

up up the mountain

still fighting forward

while the wind is

shaking me

turning me

tossing me

smacking me right in the face

over and over

again and again

the light

my only friend

my only hope

my lifeline to the shore in this ocean of
frozen sadness

made from madness

until

it's cut and gone

all of a sudden

gone

shocked

I am stumbling

crashing into a wall

that wasn't there

just a moment before

dazed

confused

I look up

there are feet

there are legs

there are arms with big hands

there are eyes

and there is

a mouth

chewing and smiling

a light shining through its teeth

but my dream

I say

is just a dream

the chewing mouth says

smiling

just a dream

devasted

I watch the mouth swallow

yummy

it says grinning and starts

to turn away

but my dream

I cry

was yummy nonetheless

it says

walking away

but my dream

I must

follow my dream

I scream

the dream eater stops

turns

around and looks at me

considering me for a moment

he says

you bugs

funny people you

are

following your dream

you must

you say

then maybe you

should follow it then

I guess

he says laughing

dreaming

there you are

she said

her face hovering over mine

waking up

all I could do was stare

her face hovering over mine

just inches away

glowing

but cast in shadows

from a fire next to us

are you really there

I said

my voice just a whisper

her lips parted in

a smile

you followed

your dream

she said

you followed

me

you are really there are you

I whispered

you are really here with me are you

are you

are

you

of course

silly

she laughed

you followed

your dream

she said

you followed me

she said

caressing my cheek

with her hand

so gentle it hurt

and here I am

living your

dream

she said

planting a kiss

on my rough lips

so light it burnt

right through my heart

live your dream

she said

embracing me

welcoming

me

in

hollowed embers

cold as desire

our love

an all-consuming fire

burning up

all compassion

before

easing up

into a gentle passion

afterwards

I was holding her

close to my heart

so close so very

very close

a heart

full of happiness

clinging to her

while she was snuggling into me

but something

felt wrong

you feel hollowed

I whispered into

a growing darkness

you followed

me

you followed

your dream

she said growing smaller and smaller

you fulfilled your

dream

you fulfilled

me

she said growing quieter and quieter

falling silent

while

the last ember of the fire

broke in two

sending sparks flying

before

flickering out

fading away

for good

forever

casting me into

an infinite void of limitless emptiness

falling

jump start

embraced

by cold emptiness

I wake up

staring at the ceiling

trying to fathom the all devouring darkness

spreading to my heart

trying to endure the silence

left behind

by her

I can still hear her voice

though

go deeper

and follow the reaper

to where dead angles lie

fly high

reach for the sky

and never say die

I traveled

far

I traveled

wide

my heart is

a patchwork of many places

but still I go

on and on

trying to catch your smile

the coastline

of my everlasting longing

the horizon

of my never-ending pain

trying to find you

love of my life

I jump up

and run

choice (crossroads – reprise)

the storm

has passed

leaving behind

its cold

leaving behind

a bright blue sky

with an even brighter shining sun

standing on the mountain ridge

I look into the sun

I only see your smile

I turn away

and look down

the fjord is still

covered in ice

the ship and its men nowhere

to be seen

crushed to dust

by the ice

I turn away

towards the corpse of the dream eater

the fallen angel

the big beast

slain

tomb of a dream

fulfilled

looking into the sun again

I spread my wings

to soar up

sky high

but a sudden breeze

approaches me

whispers in my ear

urging me to follow a path

down the other side of the mountain ridge

instead

a path

towards a village in a far distant valley

for a moment

I pause

for just a moment

I only see her smile

again

it's all I want to see

for just a moment

then I shed the memory

like I shed my wings

and

move on

Credits

비]

Idea: on the 15th of June 2018.

Written (analogue): between the 15th and the 26th of June 2018 in Seoul.

Written (digital): between the 25th and the 26th of June 2018 in Seoul.

self-mutilation

Idea: 14th of January 2019.

Written (analogue): between the 14th and the 29th of January 2019 in Seoul, Incheon, Abu Dhabi, Oberhausen and Herne.

Written (digital): between the 25th and the 30th of January 2019 in Kaiserslautern, Herne and Düsseldorf.

Snow.Falling

A Sacrifice

Idea: on the 24th of November 2018.

Written (analogue): between the 24th of November 2018 and the 1st of December 2018 in Seoul.

Written (digital): between the 1st and the 2nd of December 2018 in Seoul.

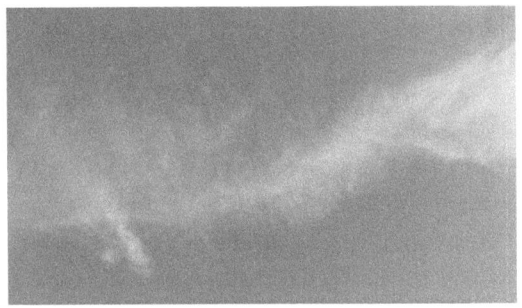

Thanks...

... to the National Museum of Korea, to the exhibitions "Goryeo: The Glory of Korea" and "Kazakhstan: The Cradleland of the 'Golden Man'"; to the writers Catherynne M. Valente, James A. Michener, Richard Mason, James Clavell, Simon Schama, Jill Santopolo, Hwang Sok-Yong, Robert I. Hellyer, Samuel Hawley, Kazuo Ishiguro, Neil Gaiman, Rainer Maria Rilke and to Veronica Roth; to the movies "The Cakemaker", "The Isle of Dogs", "Ayla", "Evergreen Love", "Valerian And The City Of A Thousand Planets" (and its soundtrack), "Frozen", "The Huntsman: Winter's War", "Beautiful Days" (animation), "Beautiful Days" (live-action), "Plonger", "A Star Is Born" (plus its soundtrack), "Aquaman", "The Dude In Me", "The Harmonium in My Memory", "Mirai", "Traces of Sin", "Every Day A Good Day", "Love Actually", "Notting Hill", "The Wolf Brigade"/ "Jin-Roh", "Hotel Transylvania", "ROMA" and to "Virgin Snow"; to the bands and musicians Leonard Cohen, Black Sabbath, Opeth, Dimmu Borgir, Behemoth, Camel, Chris Rea, Prong, Iron & Wine, Arch Enemy, Ryuichi Sakamoto, The Gazette, Britney Spears, Against The Current, Bill

Conti, SmackSoft, Symphony X, Runemagick, Dissection, Iron Maiden, L7, Free, Curved Air, Deep Purple, Dio and to Jethro Tull; to What The Book? (Seoul); to the coffee shops I'm Home (Seoul), Caffe On The Plan (Seoul), Café Kultur (OB), Café Royal (KL) and to the Literaturhaus Herne Ruhr (Koethers & Röttsches); to Wein & Spezialitäten Martina Vössing (HER); to Bärbel Wiggers, Judit & Frank Coros, Anne Weller, Fred Liebenberg, Robert Lawrence, Silke & Winfried Hahn, Klaus Marquardt & Vera Stallmann, Dr. Joachim Wittkowski, Prof. Dr. Heinz H. Menge, Dr. Hildegard Niederschlag & Detlef Wagenschütz and to Christine Grüger and to Adnan Alam.